THE CONCEPT OF JUDICIAL ACTIVISM:

ITS NATURE AND FUNCTION IN UNITED STATES CONSTITUTIONAL LAW

RONALD EDWARD
FISHER

FIRST EDITION

Manufactured in the United States of America.

ISBN 0-89491-002-7
ISBN 0-89491-003-5
Library of Congress Catalog Card Number:
77-70447

BANNER BOOKS INTERNATIONAL
13415 Ventura Boulevard
Sherman Oaks, California 91423

DEDICATION

This book is dedicated to the late Supreme Court Justice Hugo L. Black, who one day in May, 1969 set me correct in my thinking about a nebulous concept called "judicial activism."

It is also dedicated to the late Norman J. Small, professor of Constitutional Law, Howard University, who one day in the Fall of 1967 supplied me with the words "judicial activism" as a researchable concept in Constitutional Law.

The pedagogy of Professor Morris J. Levitt, Department of Political Science, Howard University, always will be remembered. But it was to take the methodology and the academic perseverance of Professor Nikolaos Stavrou, also of the Howard University Department of Political Science, to provide the direction of the research as well as meaning for the data gathered from the survey of five major colleges in Washington, D.C.

Finally, this writer's own role, as well as presence of mind, in the research of this study to its conclusion is perhaps best illustrated by the following analogous account. A young Air Force second lieutenant was about to meet a board of officers convened to interview applicants for commissions in the regular service. He had spent all of the previous evening shining his shoes, polishing his brass, and preparing for all of the questions that he might be asked. When the fateful hour arrived, he was prepared for anything—that is, anything but the higher than usual door sill. To the colonels and majors comprising the board, the young officer sprawled unceremoniously before them seemed to present a hopeless case. The lieutenant rose, however, and brushing off his neatly-pressed uniform, said with a sigh, "Well, at least I fell into good company." He received his regular commission.

To all my readers, I wish wisdom, good health, and good company!

— Ronald Edward Fisher

May, 1977

TABLE OF CONTENTS

INTRODUCTION		**1**
CHAPTER I.	**THE CONCEPT OF JUDICIAL ACTIVISM: ITS NATURE**	**7**
	Judicial Activism in a Contemporary Setting	
	The Legal and Philosophical Basis for the Nature of Judicial Activism	
CHAPTER II.	**THE CONCEPT OF JUDICIAL ACTIVISM: ITS FUNCTION**	**19**
	Judicial Activism and the "Rule of Four"	
	Judicial Activism and Certiorari	
	Judicial Restraint: The Nemesis of Judicial Activism	
CHAPTER III.	**EMPIRICAL ANALYSIS OF JUDICIAL ACTIVISM**	**29**
	Design of the Questionnaire	
	Results of the Empirical Survey	
CONCLUSION		**33**
DOCUMENTATION		**41**
SELECTED BIBLIOGRAPHY		**47**

TABLE OF ILLUSTRATIONS

1. The Judicial Conversion Function: Internal and External Influences Upon and Within the Court **12**

2. The Eleven Federal Judicial Circuits **21**

3. Dynamics of the Internal and External Effects of United States Supreme Court Decisions **23**

4. Questionnaire Design for Empirical Analysis of the Nature and Function of the Concept of Judicial Activism **30**

5. Quantified Results of Survey **34**

INTRODUCTION

This study is an investigation into the nature and function of the concept of *judicial activism* within United States Constitutional law. It was conducted to determine the ramifications and influence of this concept on the administration of the nation's judicial and legal system as a whole.

Existing interpretations of the concept of judicial activism by legal scholars and analysts of our nation's Judiciary appear to be more closely linked to "legal philosophy" within the U.S. judicial and legal system than to social dynamics. This study, however, examines the concept of judicial activism with a view of its relation to the *tri-parti*, or balanced, political structure as it exists within the United States today. The author selected this approach in an effort to interest a broader cross-section of students and other readers than have the technical legal studies produced on this subject. At the same time, the investigation conducted herein is from the vantage point of the Judiciary. Indeed, the United States Supreme Court, as the final authority within the Judiciary, is the primary institution of examination, since its decisions affect policy on "all matters of law and equity arising under this Constitution."

The Supreme Court also was chosen as the focal point of investigation because it is the institution of *original* jurisdiction in matters "both as to law and fact," especially in cases in which the United States of America is a party. *Original jurisdiction*, as used in these pages, denotes those inherent powers granted to the Supreme Court by Congress when the scope of judicial authority was set forth in Article Three of the United States Constitution. From this source, the Supreme Court was granted the powers of original jurisdiction in four major areas: (1) criminal cases; (2) cases concerning the District of Columbia; (3) review and enforcement of administrative orders; and (4) civil actions. From this, we can see that the power and jurisdiction of the Supreme Court are substantial indeed.

In this study, we also shall see that what was formerly regarded as the Court's "encroachment on the power of other branches of government" or its "expansion of ground-breaking precedent" were actually instances in which the Court exercised its powers of original jurisdiction. Supporting this, an examination of existing works on the subject is conducted to determine the prevailing perceptions of the concept of judicial activism among both legal and non-legal scholars.

Thus, the primary objectives of this study are to determine, with regard to the concept of judicial activism: (1) the nature and perception of the concept among legal and non-legal scholars; (2) the relationship between this concept and the behavior of the nation's Judiciary; (3) the relevance and functional relationship of this concept to the opposite concept of *judicial restraint*; and (4) the impact, if any, of the concept of judicial activism upon the nation's society, as measured by a survey of members of the academic community within metropolitan Washington, D.C.

In keeping with the theoretical perspectives of this study, the author views the concerted actions of both judicial activism and judicial restraint as efforts by the Supreme Court of the United States to give a balanced interpretation to its policy formulations and decisions.

Judicial restraint, as the central focus of that balance, is seen as the "nemesis" to judicial activism because the minority opinion of at least one Supreme Court Justice may, at a later time, become the majority opinion of the Court. This is illustrated in the case of *Plessy vs. Ferguson* (1893), in which a majority of the Justices voted in favor of the doctrine of "separate but equal" while the one Justice of the minority voted against it. Sixty-one years later, the minority opinion expressed in the *Plessy* case became the majority opinion of the Supreme Court in the case of *Brown vs. the School Board of Topeka, Kansas.* See *Cases*.) This tendency to adopt the minority opinion, over time, as the majority opinion has been recurrent within the Supreme Court.

The working definition of *judicial activism* for the purposes of this study is "any Constitutional interpretation by the Supreme Court of the United States, within its power of original jurisdiction, in any case in which it decides, makes a policy formulation, or a ruling by a majority or minority of the Court."

Conversely, *judicial restraint* is defined as "the limitation on any Constitutional interpretation by the Supreme Court of the United States, within its power of original jurisdiction, in any case in which it decides, makes a policy formulation, or a ruling, by a majority or minority of the Court."

Source material used in this study was drawn from: legal documents and other scholarly works relevant to the investigation; an interview with the late Mr. Justice Hugo L. Black of the United States Supreme Court; and responses to questionnaires supplied by select groups of professors and students of political science at five major universities in metropolitan Washington, D.C.: American University, Catholic University of America, George Washington University, Georgetown University, and Howard University.

This author has not relied upon textbooks for a conceptual analysis of the concept of judicial activism, as is often the case, since examination of relevant works revealed them to be limited in their scope and perception of the subject. Research by this author also confirmed that greater emphasis is now being placed on recent empirical findings pertinent to the concept of judicial activism than previously.

The very nature and scope of this study as well as the limited availability of sources and other delimitations disallow extensive treatment of the subject. Yet, in a work of this sort, one is necessarily indebted to a number of people for their singular aid and support. The writer was especially fortunate to have been granted a two-hour interview with the late Hugo L. Black, Justice of the United States Supreme Court. Reflective thanks also go to the author's maternal grandmother, whose wisdom and mental acuity contributed important support to the project. Similarly, deep appreciation is given to the very special one and the special many who provided all types of needed assistance during the course of the study. They include Emmitt C. Dorsey, former Chairman of the Department of Political Science at Howard University, who encouraged the author's interest in "Constitutional law and things that matter." My thanks as well to Professor Norman J. Small, formerly of the Department of Political Science, Howard University, and the American Law Division of the Library of Congress, who provided the suggestion for research into the concept of judicial activism during his Constitutional law class in Fall, 1967.

My special appreciation goes to Professors Nikolaos Stavrou, Babalola Cole, and Maurice Woodard of the Department of Political Science at Howard University for providing vital and constructive criticism throughout the development of this study, and for comprising a patient and objective committee for this purpose. Without the valuable aid of Professor Stavrou in providing the framework for the judicial process questionnaire to elicit "...honest, not directed answers from people not well versed in law and legal aspects...", the author may not have been able to conduct a sound and methodical empirical survey such as the one that provided the basis for this research.

Most especially, my personal gratitude goes to my brother, William V. Fisher, Jr., and my wife, Mrs. Carolyn B. Fisher, both of whom assisted infinitely and greatly to sustain the way for the ultimate completion of the research. Thank you as well to Ms. Cathy Miller, student at George Washington University, whose skillful help greatly facilitated the administration of the research questionnaires used in this study.

Particular appreciation must be reserved for the 15 professors and 108 graduate and undergraduate students at five major universities in metropolitan Washington, D.C., who graciously consented to contribute their classroom time and academic opinions to the empirical survey that provided the research data for this study. To protect the pledge of anonymity made by the author to these and other educators polled during the survey, they will be cited only as an "aggregate response group" in these pages. Similarly, all of the 108 students who responded to the questionnaire will remain unnamed.

To these and all others instrumental in the achievement of this work, my sincere appreciation.

Ronald Edward Fisher

CHAPTER I

THE CONCEPT OF JUDICIAL ACTIVISM: ITS NATURE

The concept of judicial activism is directly linked to the Supreme Court and its power within its realm of original jurisdiction. Given such a technical link, some observers of the Court's constitutional interpretations have claimed judicial activism to be an actual "legal philosophy" of the Court. Accordingly, they see evidence of judicial activism in any constitutional decision which gives the appearance of being beyond the purview of the Court's jurisdiction. The outright claim is that the Court is "legislating", and that it is encroaching on the roles of the congressional and executive branches of the federal government. While it may be true that the Court does establish ground-breaking precedent, the charges that it "legislates" and "encroaches on other branches" may warrant further examination.

Writers and scholars who see the Supreme Court as legislating and encroaching also include in their charge the view of the Supreme Court Judge as a substantive factor within the judicial and legal process. Professor William F. Swindler writes of this charge by court critics claiming a connection between judicial attitude and judicial activism. Specifically, he states: "...for the activists the question of legislative inaction required a judicial inquiry into the existence of a governmental obligation implicit in the Constitution ..."[1]

Scholars as well as non-legal court observers continue to have difficulty defining the line of demarcation between "legislating" and "interpreting" in Court policies and decisions. Professor Wallace Mendelson concludes that confusion on the point is caused by the Court's use of its "discretion," an inherent power derived from a congressional grant more than fifty years ago. Professor Mendelson aptly observes:

> How much law and how much discretion (or justice) are appropriate in the decision of a concrete case? What are the proper proportions in each of the myriad contexts in which a court must resolve the discrepancy between the generic directives of the law and the unanticipated, or imperfectly foreseen, controversies that demand adjudication? This is the basic problem in the judicial process. A tendency one way rather than the other is the difference between our "activists" and our more self-respecting judges.
>
> The written Constitution of course, does not avoid the basic difficulty. It comes to us, after all, out of the eighteenth century. It was written by men wise enough to know they could not prescribe the details of policy for an "undefined and expanding future." Nor were they in complete accord among themselves on vital issues — just as we are not. And so for the most part they wrote not only in generalities but often in calculated evasion of crucial issues. In short, the Founding Fathers, and the amenders as well, avoided strait-jacketing precision. Their forte was the suggestive, open-ended hint. That is why the Constitution has survived when other works of its age — in medicine, engineering, physics, and what not — have long since passed away.
>
> The Constitution lives on in a changing world because it grows not only by formal amendment but also by "interpretation" — a process in which the judiciary plays a large, yet by no means an exclusive role. Lawmaking, then, is an inherent and inevitable part of the judicial process. Judges must be more than mimics. Greatness on the bench — or elsewhere — lies in creativity.[2]

Similarly, Lon Fuller, in his work, *The Law in Quest of Itself*, raises the pertinent question: "Just what do we mean by a judge's 'actions' as distinguished from his meaning and intentions"?[3] This, too, points to the difficulty of definitions. Obviously a judge's "actions" derive chiefly from his own perception of the facts. Thus, the judge's perception serves to produce his decision, which must be within the framework of a constitutionally prescribed area. No Justice can "act" beyond the bounds of the Constitution and continue to have his decisions rest validly within constitutional jurisprudence, as established firmly within the American judicial and legal process. The working definition of *Judicial activism* set forth in this study clearly constrains the behavior of a Justice to constitutionally prescribed limits. Were a Justice to engage in an act outside the limits imposed by the Constitution on his "actions", a different type of charge would ensue — one that would permit his dismissal for "improper" conduct.

The idea of a constitution is one of man making a "compact" with his fellow man, as envisioned by the "social contract thinkers."[4] This "compact" is actually another name for "constitution." A "constitution" or "compact" is written with regard for basic human rights and norms that each member would obey to support mutual allegiance and to preserve society.

The United States Constitution was the product not only of the writings of the colonial leaders, but was drafted to include portions of several other compacts, some of which were written centuries before it.[5] For example, the United States Constitution contains some of the elements of the *Magna Carta*: when Chief Justice John Marshall, in the 1803 Supreme Court case of *Maubury vs. Madison*, asserted the Constitution was "the fundamental law of the land", he was repeating a principle declared centuries earlier in the *Magna Carta*.[6]

In a personal interview with the author, the late Mr. Justice Hugo L. Black addressed the question of judicial activism within the framework of constitutional jurisprudence. Justice Black stated that he based his faith in the Supreme Court's ability to interpret the United States Constitution as a living document on two personal convictions: (1) his enduring belief in the Bill of Rights, and (2) his belief that there existed "absolutes" in the Constitution of the United States.[7] At the same time, Justice Black admonished the author to be wary of concepts which lack substance, pointing again to the difficulty of defining the discretionary powers of the Supreme Court.[8]

The concept of "absolute" raised by Mr. Justice Black will not be explored in these pages, nor will an *en bloc* examination be made of the Bill of Rights. While both are pertinent to the concept of judicial activism, their inclusion would make this study more extensive than intended for the area of investigation prescribed. However, within the framework of the research, the author has proceeded on the assumption that both elements were a part of the essential means which enabled the United States Constitution to remain a living document.

A degree of confusion attends the concept of judicial activism, even within the area of "discretion" discussed by Professor Mendelson. The first judicial authority to write on the concept of judicial activism per se was Judge Skelly Wright. In his major work on the subject, Judge Wright states: "Its active role in shaping our society has been a necessary and proper one... The need for judicial action is strongest in the areas of the law where political process proves inadequate, not from lack of legislative power but because the problem is neglected by politicians."[9]

In a similar spirit, and to show his source for a historical basis for judicial activism, as well as to indicate that the concept does indeed have substance, Professor Alpheus T. Mason cited the 1893 address of the late Mr. Justice Brewer before the New York Bar Association, wherein he proclaimed: "Strengthen the Judiciary!"[10]

As stated earlier, judicial activism is directly linked to the Supreme Court and its power within the realm of its original jurisdiction. In some of the foregoing citations, judges and scholars appear to suggest that judicial activism may properly go beyond the constitutional limitations as set forth in our working definition, so as to achieve an active and creative role for a Justice. To some, the term "creative" means "legislating", a role clearly assigned to Congress. However, the basis of the Court's inherent power is derived from a Congressional grant through the Twenty-fifth Section of the Judiciary Act of 1789, the following excerpt of which describes the impact of the historical section:

> 'Since its adoption in 1789, the Twenty-fifth Section of that Act, which granted to the United States Supreme Court a limited jurisdiction on appeal from decisions of State courts, has never been materially changed. This jurisdiction is now practically confined to cases where a State court has decided in favor of the constitutionality of a State law or proceeding.[11]

Within the context of this chapter, we can see that there are many aspects to the concept of judicial activism which are relevant to its nature. The concept appears to be a part of "external" influences upon the Court as an institution, and a part of "internal" influences upon Supreme Court Justices to produce a vote in one direction or the other. In the empirical segment of this work, both areas will be analyzed to determine which has the greater import for the existence of judicial activism. Some scholars have appropriately called this phenomenon "the judicial conversion function." The author has concluded, however, that, instead of a judicial *inversion* function upon and within the Court as an influence, the actual process, as it relates to the nature of judicial activism, is indeed a judicial *conversion* function; i.e., with both internal and external influences acting as indeterminable influences upon the judge's decision to vote one way or the other.

An initial conception of the judicial conversion function is illustrated in **Figure 1.** The circle in the right of the rectangle represents the author's conception of the internal and external influences upon the Court and one Justice, as an example of how the same process could be at work on the other eight Justices of the United States Supreme Court. **Figure 1** Also shows influences within the Court structure which may serve to affect a Justice's vote. In Chapters II and III, these internal influences will be analyzed in some detail. The vote, which could be a decision either for or against the facts within a case or the law upon which the case is brought before the Court for review, is indicated by the circled "V" on the left side of the rectangle.

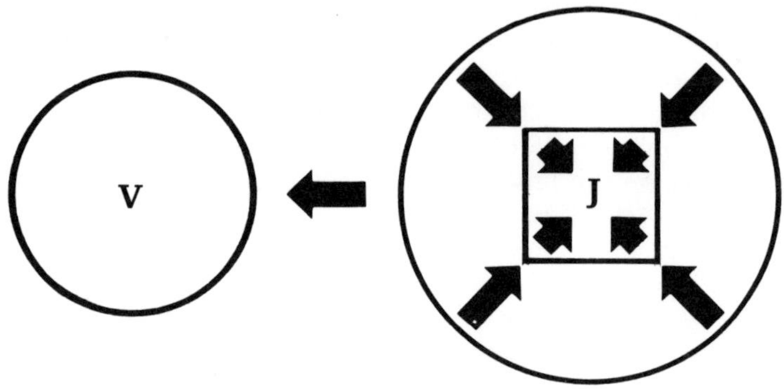

J = Any judge within any given court structure, although the usual focus is upon the United States Supreme Court.

V = A judge's final vote in a given case.

➧ = All arrows within the box indicate internal influences upon the conversion function. The arrows outside of the box indicate external influences upon the conversion function. The longer arrow between the two circles is the summation arrow. It indicates any group of influences producing any one vote in a given court structure.

Fig. 1. The Judicial Conversion Function: Internal and External Influences upon and within the Court.

JUDICIAL ACTIVISM IN A CONTEMPORARY SETTING

Figure 1 illustrates the author's conceptualization of the judicial conversion function. We see that judicial conversion is composed of external and internal influences upon and within the Court. As concrete examples, we may consider the verbal arguments of counsel and the personal persuasion of other Justices within the Friday conference as internal influences, and the writings by legal and non-legal scholars, and as some charge, "the headlines of the *New York Times*," as external influences.

At this writing the first Session of the Ninety-Third Congress is convened. A major issue facing the members of Congress is that of *executive privilege*. The concept of executive privilege is a matter which ultimately may be decided in the Supreme Court of the United States. To date, no litigation has been initiated to determine the proper limits and scope of this controversial concept. But were this matter presented to the Supreme Court for decision, the Court would have the power to decide it, since it is a matter within original jurisdiction of the Court.

As a Congressional issue, the attorneys for Congress could make the following arguments against the present use of executive privilege: (1) the Executive ought not be allowed to maintain, like its predecessors, that its orders and conversations are privileged, as well as those of all other members of the expanded White House staff; (2) the scope of executive privilege ought not be extended to afford blanket coverage to former employees of the Executive; and (3) the Executive should be prohibited from maintaining that the concept covers not only conversations that have to do with decisions and matters of policy within the Executive, but also extends to protect criminal conduct.

The attorneys for the Executive could then argue that executive privilege necessarily extends to anyone employed within the Executive because everyone in that branch of government does the work of the President; and, the attorneys could maintain that the matter of criminal conduct has yet to be proved.[12]

The author believes that, if the matter of executive privilege became an issue for the Supreme Court to decide, it would most likely arrive at a decision in such a manner as to avoid a constitutional confrontation, since such a confrontation could damage the principle of "separation of powers" as it exists in the

American governmental and legal system. But, ideally, should the Court decide the case on its merits, which it has the power to do under its original jurisdiction, it could decide that there is not an "absolute" scope to executive privilege, but that there is a "limited" one, which the Court might then be inclined to delineate.

In Chapter II, we shall see how the composition of the Court often has a decisive influence on the way in which it decides a particular case, making its composition an "internal" factor affecting a Justice's rulings. The composition of the present Court is favorably disposed to the policies of the Executive Branch. Therefore, should an issue like executive privilege be presented to the Court for decision, it may not be prudent to believe the issue will be decided on its own merits.

This writer proposes that although judicial activism may appear to be the *immediate process* of a judicial action, it may, in fact, be the *immediate effect*. For example, we may sit in on a hearing of the Supreme Court at any time it is in public session. Should we return the following Monday, we would hear the results of the Justices' Friday deliberations. But are we really witnessing a "weekend decision"? What we may in fact, be witnessing is the immediate effect of a "judicial predisposition" or "legal policy" that the Court may well have settled upon years or even decades before. Therefore, what seems contemporary to the Court could well be an issue of precedent spanning decades. For example, the work of one legal scholar shows the precedent for the modern roots of judicial activism was established in 1937, which means the concept was espoused nearly forty years ago.[13]

Melvin Wulf, the Legal Director of the American Civil Liberties Union, wrote in an article in its newspaper, *Civil Liberties*, "Regardless of the social and political instincts of any of the Justices, they are all lawyers with roots that go deep into the traditions of the legal system, which is itself profoundly conservative."[14] Wulf concluded: "The good decisions could only be seen as temporary aberrations which will predictably decrease as time goes on and as the new Justices work their way into their roles."[15]

Some writers see the Justices' "working their way into their roles" as a matter of "personal activism" for each of them, so that such varieties of activism could be readily identified. For example, Columnist John P. MacKenzie wrote "...the Burger Court has furthered a recent trend of judicial activism which could blossom into what the Warren Court critics feared — government by the Judiciary. There would be one difference: conservative judges would be in command. Still, the only question would be whose brand of judicial activism you prefer."[16]

THE LEGAL AND PHILOSOPHICAL BASES FOR THE NATURE OF JUDICIAL ACTIVISM

There are at least four points upon which to base a case in which the United States Supreme Court does not legislate or encroach on the other branches of government. However, all of these four points could indicate that the Court may establish ground-breaking precedent.

The first point is one cited by the Court in the *Carolene Products* Case: "...whether prejudice against discrete and insular minorities may be a special condition, which tends seriously to curtail the operation of those political processes ordinarily to be relied upon to protect minorities, and which may call for a correspondingly more searching judicial inquiry."[17]

A second major point disproving Court legislation and encroachment is found in *The Judiciary Act of 1789*, passed during the First Congress, the Twenty-Fifth Section of which elucidated and expanded the power of the Court.[18]

The third major point which disproves legislation and encroachment by the Court derives from the primary source of judicial power, *The United States Constitution, Article III*.[19] As stated earlier, the author believes no case may be cited as evidence that the Supreme Court has gone beyond its Congressionally mandated powers as set forth in that Article.

The following citation shows that critics of the Supreme Court have improperly confused Court legislation and Court encroachment with the "interpretive" power duly granted to the Court by Congress:

> Judicial Power, as Justice Miller defined it in 1891, is the power "of a court to decide and pronounce a judgment and carry it into effect between persons and parties who bring a case before it for decision"...Although the terms "judicial power" and "jurisdiction" are frequently used interchangeably and

> jurisdiction is defined as the power to hear and determine the subject matter in controversy between parties to a suit, or as the "power to entertain the suit, consider the merits and render a binding decision thereon," the cases and commentaries support and, for that matter, necessitate a distinction between the two concepts. Jurisdiction is the authority of a court to exercise judicial power in a specific case and is, of course, a prerequisite to the exercise of judicial power, which is the totality of powers a court exercises when it assumes jurisdiction and hears and decides a case.[20]

To avoid confusion between the Court's power and its jurisdiction, the following citation is provided, an excerpt from an Annotation of the Constitution prepared by the American Law Division of the Library of Congress:

> The distinction between judicial power and jurisdiction is especially pertinent to the meaning of the words "shall be vested." Whereas all of the judicial power of the United States is vested in the Supreme Court and the lower federal judiciary, neither has ever been vested with all the jurisdiction they are capable of receiving under Article III. Except for the original jurisdiction of the Supreme Court, which flows directly from the Constitution, two prerequisites to jurisdiction must be present. First, the Constitution must have given the courts the capacity to receive it; second, an act of Congress must have conferred it.[21]

The fourth point to counter accusations of Court legislation or encroachment is found in the so-called "Judges' Bill" of 1925. This bill, which became an act, is important to an understanding of the nature of judicial activism because, prior to 1925, and for a period of 35 years the Court and Congress had been at a crossroads. Research shows that volumes of appellate cases were being presented to the Court for decision. Critical judicial matters began to take the Court an inordinate amount of time to settle. Overworked Justices were at odds with their tasks as judges. There was a drastic need for internal restructuring of the Court. But the Court's ability to restructure itself on its own behalf was restricted by congressional statute.

Prior to 1925, the United States Supreme Court had no "discretion" over direct appeal cases which came before it. To correct this, the members of the Court made an exasperated request to Congress for relief. As a result, the bill introduced into Congress by the judges of the Supreme Court themselves was called the Judges' Bill.[22] This bill gave the Court another of its inherent powers: the power to grant *Certiorari* in cases which came before it. Once the Court was granted the Certiorari power by Congress, it obtained the power of discretion.[23]

CHAPTER II

THE CONCEPT OF JUDICIAL ACTIVISM: ITS FUNCTION

JUDICIAL ACTIVISM AND THE "RULE OF FOUR"

Within this chapter, the function of judicial activism will be examined with regard to four main related aspects: (1) the "Rule of Four"; (2) 5-to-4 Decisions of the United States Supreme Court and their effect on the Court's image; (3) the concept of Certiorari as it related to the function of judicial activism; and (4) judicial restraint, the "nemesis" of judicial activism as a delimiter on its scope. These four judicial elements comprise part of the basis for the function of judicial activism.

The "Rule of Four" essentially identifies the manner in which a case is taken into consideration by the full Supreme Court, generally all nine members. Specifically, it holds that four Justices of the Court must agree among themselves that a case before them contains a substantial federal or constitutional question, one which should be further considered on its merits during verbal argument before the Court. Such a review, of course, is an inherent right of the Court.

Some scholars and journalists have maintained there is significance in the decision of whether or not to grant Certiorari to a petition before the Court. Certain scholars argue further that a petition returned "Certiorari Denied" has a substantive implication. A "Certiorari Denied" petition is one which has been rejected after a review by the Court. Usually, it has been found not to have substantial constitutional merit. This means, of course, that the Supreme Court has affirmed the decision of the court below, which coincides with the claim made by scholars and journalists.[24] On this point, the Rules of the Supreme Court of the

United States explain the Court's consideration(s) for Certiorari:

> 1. The petition for writ of certiorari shall contain in the order here indicated —
>
> (a) A reference to the official and unofficial reports of the opinions delivered in the courts below, if any, and if reported.
>
> (b) A concise statement of the grounds on which the jurisdiction of this court is invoked, showing:
>
> (i) The date of the judgment or decree sought to be reviewed, and the time of its entry;
>
> (ii) The date of any order respecting a rehearing, and the date and terms of any order granting an extension of time within which to petition for certiorari; and
>
> (iii) The statutory provision believed to confer on this court jurisdiction to review the judgment or decree in question by writ of certiorari...
>
> (c) The questions presented for review, expressed in the terms and circumstances of the case but without unnecessary detail;
>
> (d) The constitutional provisions, treaties, statutes, ordinances, or regulations which the case involves, setting them out verbatim, and citing the volume and page where they may be found in the official edition....
>
> ....
>
> 4. The failure of a petitioner to present with accuracy, brevity, and clearness whatever is essential to a ready and adequate understanding of the points requiring consideration will be a sufficient reason for denying his petition...[25]

Congressional statute is the authority upon which the Supreme Court exercises its jurisdiction over the eleven Judicial Circuits, which are illustrated in **Figure 2.** The primary basis for a petition of Certiorari is that a "substantial federal question" is held to exist. This prerequisite to the "Rule of Four" grant of Certiorari usually derives from a conflict of interpretation in at least two of the eleven Judicial Circuits. Pursuant to such a conflict, there must be two opposing rulings in the lower courts. For example, Judicial Circuit 1, which is composed of Maine, Vermont, New Hampshire, and Massachusetts, could interpret a "rule of law" or a congressional statute in one manner, while Judicial Circuit 5, which consists of Texas, Louisiana, Florida, Alabama, Georgia, and Mississippi, could interpret the rule or statute in another manner, giving rise to the conflict. It is from this kind of conflict that the Court usually will grant Certiorari through its "Rule of Four" and hear the case on its merits in the time allotted for oral argument.

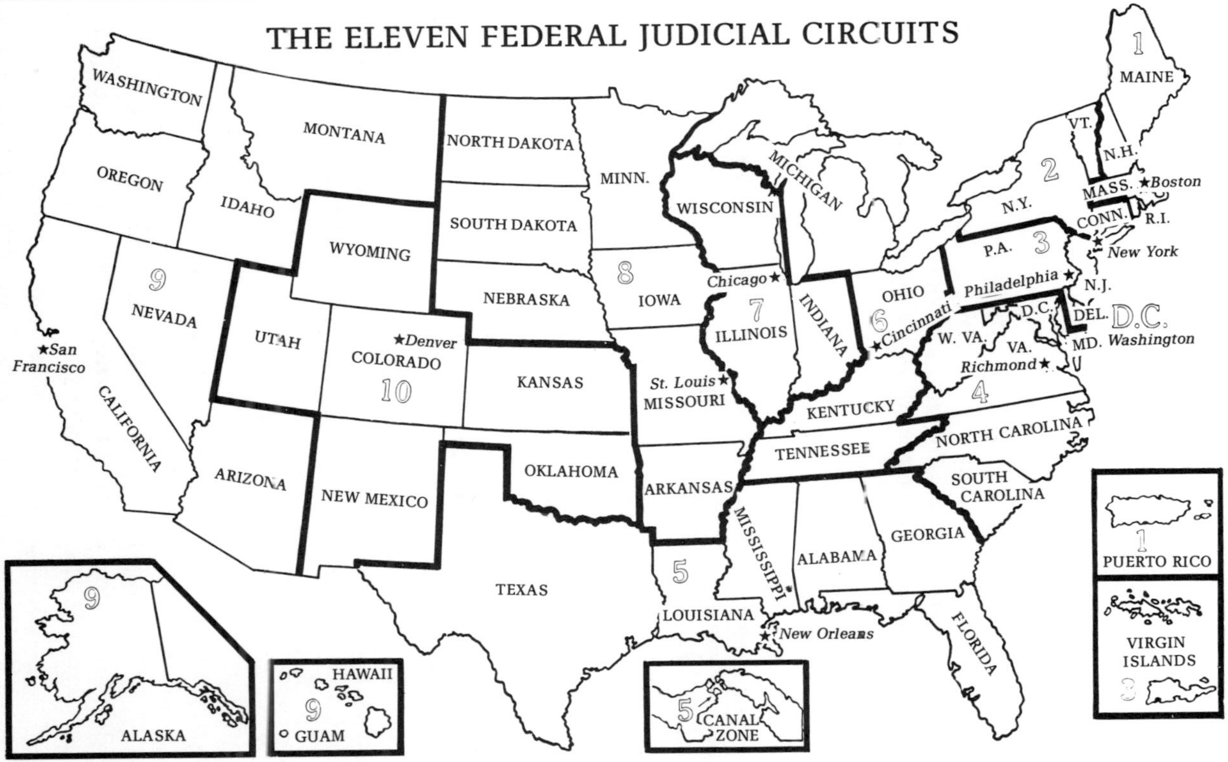

Fig. 2 Reproduced from *West's Law Finder*, 1972, p. 2, by permission of West Publishing Company, St. Paul, Minnesota.

Additionally, one such decision by the court disposing of a case involving a conflict between two circuits not only affects all of the circuits as a matter of policy, but also indicates to lower court judges a particular legal policy direction which the Supreme Court has chosen to follow.

In her article concerning the "Rule of Four" in *Columbia Law Review*, Joan Maisel Leiman states that, if five Justices oppose and four Justices are willing, then a case should be disposed of on its merits.[26] The technical point made by Ms. Leiman is that, if four Justices are willing to grant Certiorari, that in itself should be sufficient for the case to be heard on its merits before the whole Court.

As a matter of practical concern, however, such an argument has at least three defects: (1) In some instances, only three Justices "feel strongly" about the case. The fourth Justice merely casts his vote as a "courtesy" (see *Note 25*); (2) there is the assumption that the Justices' granting Certiorari upon the "Rule of Four" indicates that all of these same four Justices will ultimately vote favorably upon the case to which they granted the Certiorari petition; (3) finally, author Leiman overlooks the possibility that such verbal argument actually is an appeal to the fifth Justice for the decisive vote and a favorable ruling by the full Court. The assumption here, of course, is that, when the nine-member Court hears the case, the four Justices who granted the Certiorari petition will continue to support such a petition after hearing the verbal arguments on the merits of the case. Author Leiman further contends in her article that 5/4 decisions by the Court have caused consternation, because the image of the Court has been reduced thereby as some Justices of the lower courts "took issue with the majority's interpretation of the rule and refused to be bound by it."[27]

In the same article, Leiman cites Justice Harlan, who, in voting for a majority interpretation of the "Rule of Four", held that the rules are to be interpreted to mean "any case warranting consideration in the opinion of such a substantial minority of the Court (meaning four members) will be taken and disposed of."[28]

The late Mr. Justice Frankfurter, who was the author of the "Rule of Four", wrote "...the rule of four means only that the Court will hear a case if four of the nine Justices believe, on the basis of the petition for Certiorari, that it is one the Court should consider, but not necessarily decide."[29]

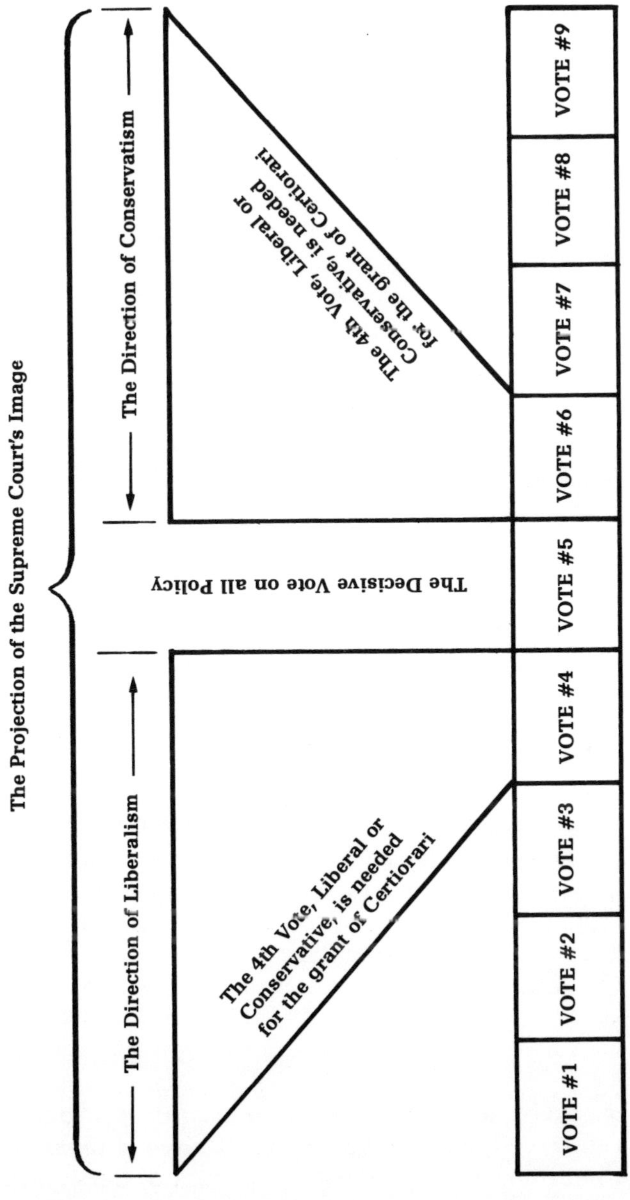

Fig. 3. Dynamics of the Internal and External Effects of United States Supreme Court Decisions.

Illustrated in **Figure 3** is the confusion surrounding the interpretation of the "Rule of Four" in a nine-member court. The diagram indicates how the "Rule of Four" is involved with court dynamics as well as the conservative-liberal image of the Court.

Also shown in **Figure 3** is how the composition of the Court can give an image of being conservative or liberal. Often, the final voting in a case can be examined and shown to reflect a conservative or liberal voting bloc on the Court.

JUDICIAL ACTIVISM AND CERTIORARI

One of the inherent legal and philosophical powers of the Supreme Court is that of Certiorari. Certiorari has its historical origin in the English Common Law heritage of *Prerogative*, where it was the "prerogative" of the king to "hear" certain pleadings.[30] No power such as "prerogative" was given to the United States Supreme Court in the Judiciary Act of 1789. As stated earlier, it was not until 1925 that the Court received the power of Certiorari from Congress. This congressional grant of power to the Court meant that the Court had "discretionary" right over some cases, whereas other cases carried automatic appeal.[31]

Another concept which bears somewhat on judicial activism is cue theory. According to its originator, Joseph Tannenhaus, cue theory holds that: "...the Justices of the Supreme Court employ cues as a means of separating those petitions worthy of scrutiny from those that may be discarded without further study."[32]

In the May, 1972 issue of the *Law and Society Review*, Sidney Ulmer et al. presented an article relevant to a functional inquiry into the concept of Certiorari. Research by the Ulmer group found that 85 to 90 percent of all applications for Court review came by way of the Certiorari. Ulmer and his associates were particularly interested in "how the Court makes its choices in this area — how it determines who receives access to its review process and who is denied..."[33]

Cue theory exists to alert a Justice to scrutinize a particular petition for certain significant questions. If none of these "cues" appear in a petition, there need not be a grant of Certiorari.

Accordingly, using the Tannenhaus study as a basis, the Ulmer group postulates the following three propositions as the substantive elements of cue theory:

(1) When the federal government, as a party, seeks review, the likelihood of Certiorari being granted is greater than when other parties seek review.

(2) When dissension has been indicated in the court immediately below, or between two or more courts and agencies in a given case, the likelihood of Certiorari being granted is greater than when such dissension is absent.

(3) When a civil liberty issue is present, the likelihood of Certiorari being granted is greater than when no civil liberty issue is present.[34]

As stated earlier in these pages, judicial activism as well as judicial restraint enable the Court to promulgate its policy formulations with an element of balance. Such balance can be seen in the concept of judicial restraint as the nemesis to judicial activism.

Judicial Restraint: The Nemesis of Judicial Activism

Judicial restraint is considered to be the nemesis of judicial activism, not only for the reasons cited earlier, but for two other substantive reasons: (1) it allows for a conservative majority or minority of four Justices on a nine-member Court to frustrate or confuse lower courts by causing dissension, as noted by author Leiman; (2) judicial restraint impedes judicial activism because of its strict reliance on precedent and on what some writers call conservative legal policy.

The policy of judicial restraint is perhaps most evident in the writings of the late Mr. Justice Felix Frankfurter. The policy of the late Justice usually was reflected in his opinions, which sought to achieve a balance between the rights of the individual and his need for privacy and the rights of the state and its need for self-preservation. Specific indications of Justice Frankfurter's philosophy can be seen in the Sweeny Case:

> To be sure, this opinion is a conclusion based on a judicial judgment in balancing two contending principles — the right of a citizen to political privacy, as protected by the Fourteenth Amendment and the right of the state to self protection. And striking the balance implies the exercise of judgment. This is the inescapable judicial task in giving substantive content, legally enforced to the due process clause, and it is a task ultimately

> committed to this Court. It must not be an exercise of whim or will. It must be an overriding judgment founded on something much deeper and more justifiable than the personal preference. As far as it lies within limitations, it must be impersonal judgment. It must rest on fundamental presuppositions rooted in history to which widespread acceptance may be fairly attributed. Such a judgment must be arrived at in a spirit of humility when it counters the judgment of the state's highest court. But in the end, judgment cannot be escaped — the judgment of this Court."[35]

The facts of the Sweeny Case have been omitted in order that emphasis may be placed upon the significance of the philosophy espoused in the case by the late Justice Frankfurter.

The central arguments for the legal policy of judicial restraint advanced by Judge Skelly Wright are:

(1) LIMITATIONS OF INSTITUTIONAL COMPETENCY: The stress here is not on the illegitimacy of the Court's behaving like a legislature, but on its incapacity to do so effectively. To begin with, we are told that the Court cannot act until a case is brought to it, and that anything said in the course of the opinion that is not crucial to the decision itself is mere dictum and without the force of law. Moreover, the judgment in a particular case binds only the parties. Consequently, the Court can never confront a broad social issue or solve it in a comprehensive fashion...

(2) ADVERSE EFFECTS ON POPULAR RESPONSIBILITY: Here the emphasis is not on the ineffectiveness of judicial action, but on the debilitating side effects such action is likely to have on the other branches of the government. For if the Court steps in to correct the constitutional errors of the legislative and executive branches of government, those institutions will come to rely on it to do so and will cease to discharge their own responsibilities to remain within the boundaries of the Constitution...

(3) THE COURT AS AN UNDEMOCRATIC INSTITUTION: A final argument for judicial restraint goes neither to the Court's efficiency nor to the effect of judicial review on other branches of government, but rather to the Court's legitimacy as a policy-maker in a democratic society. Here the Court's required self-restraint is said to follow from its undemocratic structure. The syllogism goes something like this: ours is an essentially democratic society. The Supreme Court, in its reviewing capacity, is an undemocratic, "inherently oligarchic," and "deviant institution in the American democracy." Therefore, except in the most compelling situations it should allow the representative bodies to act, or not act, as they choose.[36]

Whereas judicial activism may be regarded as the philosophy of liberalism, judicial restraint, as its nemesis, acts to stabilize judicial activism. In fact, evidence uncovered through research indicates that some authorities consider judicial restraint to be the legal policy of the technical approach to substantive and procedural issues presented to the Court.

In the chapter that follows, an empirical analysis will be presented of the perception and understanding of judicial activism among selected members of the academic community of metropolitan Washington, D.C. This community was selected for survey not only because of its unique multi-university makeup, but because its proximity to the nucleus of the Federal Government was seen as providing a research sample sensitive to matters Political and Constitutional.

CHAPTER III

EMPIRICAL ANALYSIS OF JUDICIAL ACTIVISM

DESIGN OF THE QUESTIONNAIRE

A simple quantitative analysis of the empirical findings of the research was adjudged more meaningful for purposes of this study. For this reason, specific segments of the data are quantified in this chapter to bring the findings into sharper focus.

In keeping with the requirements for significant data in any type of empirical survey, an identifiable setting had to be determined and selected as the optimum locus for the study. The university community within metropolitan Washington, D.C. was therefore selected for this survey because of the probability that its members, by virtue of their locale, more greatly identified with matters, Political and Constitutional.[37]

Figure 4 was conceived to illustrate the quantification of the results derived from the empirical survey, as well as to illustrate the comparative meanings of these results. It also reflects the intent of the author to show precisely which of the external influences, in the view of the professors and students of political science surveyed, are deemed significant for observing the nature and function of the concept of judicial activism. Additionally, **Figure 4** was designed to show which, if any, of these influences had an effect that contributed to Court action or inaction.

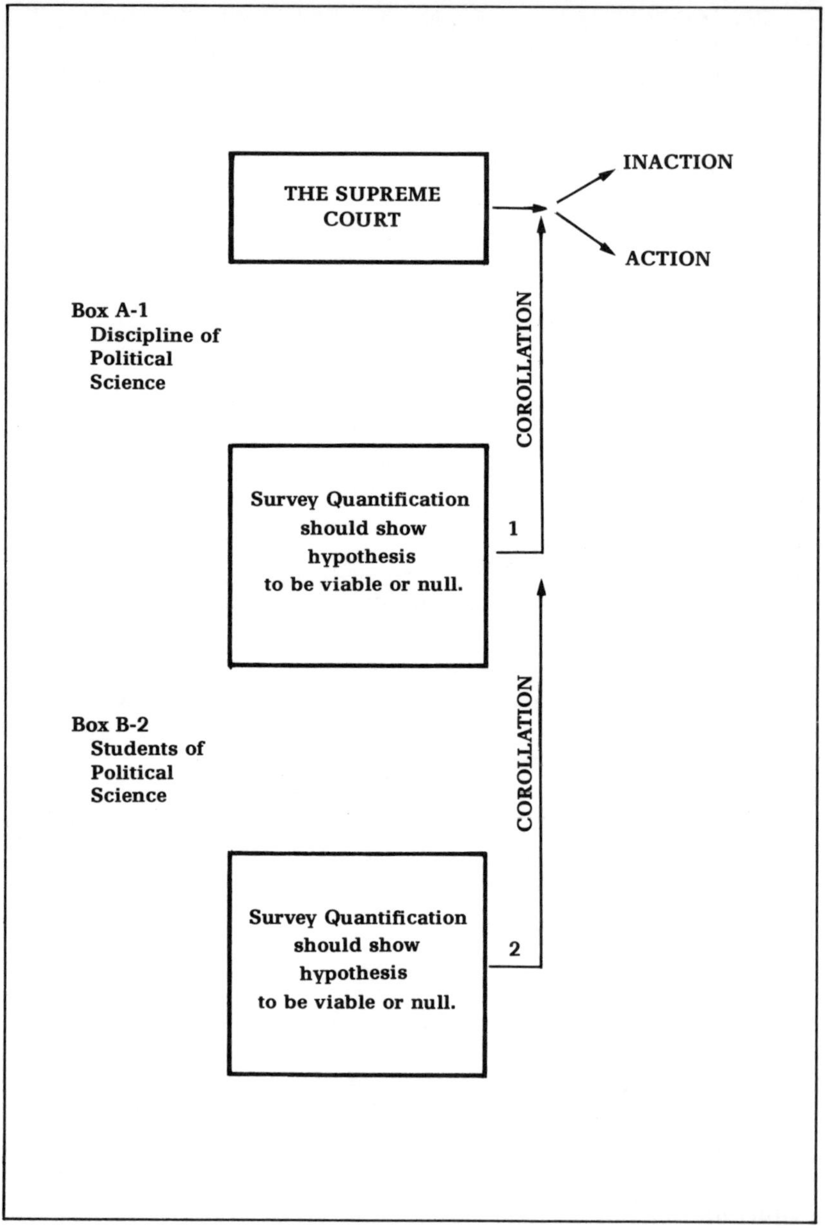

Fig. 4. Questionnaire Design for Empirical Analysis of the Nature and Function of the Concept of Judicial Activism.

EMPIRICAL ANALYSIS OF JUDICIAL ACTIVISM

The Questionnaires used for the empirical analysis of the concept of judicial activism were administered at a time adjudged to be most favorable for a survey concerning the judicial process. On November 15, 1971, when these questionnaires were distributed, the United States Senate Judiciary Committee was holding hearings on the nominations of William Rehnquist and Lewis Powell as Justices of the Supreme Court. In keeping with this noteworthy event, the political atmosphere in Washington, D.C. appeared to be conducive to an empirical survey. However, for the sake of brevity, and for their special significance, only two of the questionnaires administered are presented and analyzed here. They are:

FIRST QUESTIONNAIRE

"In your opinion, what does Judicial Activism mean?"

(A) Judicial Legislating
(B) Judicial Restraint
(C) Judicial Legal Policy
(D) Judicial Administration
(E) All of the above
(F) None of the above

SECOND QUESTIONNAIRE

"Do you think Judicial Activism is a *term* or a philosophy actually used by the Supreme Court? Or do you think it is a *term* imputed to the Supreme Court?"

(A) Imputed ______________________

(B) Used ______________________

Permission to administer these questionnaires was granted to the author by professors of political science of the five universities to whom queries were directed for the purpose of this study. The early indication was a probable response of 90 to 93 percent. The maximum possible number of respondents was 272 professors and students. Of this number, 108 professors and students responded to the questionnaires, or 39.7 percent of the total.

Accordingly, this is the number and percentage that will be used herein to represent the "aggregate response group," i.e., 108 = 100 percent.

The data, for quantification purposes, was then reduced to five independent variable categories. These categories, followed by the *shortened response* categories, are:

(1) Female Undergraduate Students of Political Science: (FUPS)

(2) Male Undergraduate Students of Political Science: (MUPS)

(3) Female Graduate Students of Political Science: (FGPS)

(4) Male Graduate Students of Political Science: (MGPS)

(5) Professors of Political Science, Graduate and Undergraduate Courses therein: (PPS)

The aggregate response categories surveyed for purposes of this study is as shown here:

Five major Washington, D.C. area universities with the respective component parts shown thereafter were surveyed. They are:

- (1) American University
  (2) Catholic University
  (3) George Washington University
  (4) Georgetown University
  (5) Howard University

- Within these five universities, only the courses which dealt with some relevant aspect of constitutional law were surveyed, in order that the results of the survey be clearly significant.
- Political Science, *Undergraduate*. Only those undergraduate Political Science courses which were directly concerned with the judicial process, constitutional law or legal policy were chosen to be surveyed.
- Political Science, *Graduate*. Only those graduate Political Science courses which were concerned with the judicial process, constitutional law or legal policy were chosen to be surveyed.
- Political Science *Professors*. Only professors who taught the aforementioned graduate and undergraduate courses concerned with judicial process, constitutional law or legal policy were surveyed.
- Political Science *Students*. Only students enrolled in the aforementioned graduate and undergraduate courses concerned with judicial process, constitutional law or legal policy were surveyed.

RESULTS OF THE EMPIRICAL SURVEY

It was assumed by the author that professors who taught at universities in the Washington, D.C. area and the students who attended these universities would be comparatively more aware of the apparatus of Federal Government and especially of the Judicial Process, the subject upon which the survey questionnaires were administered. It was further assumed that professors and students of political science in these Washington, D.C. universities would be even more cognizant of the federal governmental apparatus and the judicial process thereof. Therefore, the results from a survey concerned with these kinds of variables were believed to be significant in their findings.

The percentages and numbered tabulation of the results of the questionnaires administered to the 108 subjects for this empirical survey are delineated in **Figure 5.** From these, we can see that most of the 108 respondents to Questionnaire One thought *judicial activism* meant (A) "juicial legislating." The next most frequently cited alternative answer was a combination of judicial restraint, judicial legal policy, and judicial administration. From the tabulation of subject responses to Questionnaire Two, however, it can be seen that most of the subjects considered "judicial activism" to be a term IMPUTED to the Supreme Court.

It is of noteworthy significance that the responses to Questionnaires One and Two indicate that most of the professors and students of Political Science surveyed believed the Supreme Court to be engaged in judicial legislating. As was pointed out earlier, this, too, is a belief held by some legal and nonlegal scholars. As a reflection of the larger view of the academic community in the metropolitan Washington, D.C. area, these opinions of the subject group may indicate the existence of some confusion with regard to the function of the Supreme Court.

It can be reasoned that this confusion about the Court may exist because the Court gives the appearance of "legislating" to some who view the court through the more familiar workings of Congress. No doubt, Congress is more familiar to both members of the academic community of Washington, D.C. and to certain legal and non-legal scholars because of (1) its greater number of members; (2) the more frequent turnover of its membership; and (3) the voting right, which is inherent in United States citizenship.

RESPONSES TO QUESTIONNAIRE ONE

	FUPS	MUPS	FGPS	MGPS	PPS	
(A)	13	23	3	3	3	
(B)	—	1	—	—	—	
(C)	3	11	2	2	2	
(D)	—	—	—	—	—	
(E)	14	20	2	4	—	
(F)	—	2	—	—	—	
Total #:	30	57	7	9	5	=108
Total %:	27.7%	52.7%	5.5%	.83%	.46%	

RESPONSES TO QESTIONNAIRE TWO

		FUPS	MUPS	FGPS	MGPS	PPS	
(A)		12	20	3	3	1	
(B)		18	37	4	6	4	
Total #:		30	57	7	9	5	=108
Total %:	(A)	40%	35%	43%	33%	20%	=*Used*
	(B)	60%	65%	57%	67%	80%	=*Imputed*

Fig. 5. Quantified Results of Survey. This diagram illustrates the quantified results and the tabulation of the aggregate responses to the two questionnaires used in the empirical survey.

Perhaps some confusion about the role of the Court also exists among these groups because of the heretofore mystique surrounding certain significant aspects of the nation's Judicial Process, particularly the function of the United States Supreme Court. Some of the lesser known aspects of the Court's function were examined in Chapter II.

This author believes a mystique may be sustained by certain attitudes regarding the concept of "separation of powers" as it exists within the Federal Government. This concept usually is interpreted as identifying the three branches of government of the United States. While correct, this interpretation tends to cause confusion among observers who regard the co-equal branches of government as functioning alike. Further confusion is added when scholars and other observers attribute the function of policymaking to all three branches of Federal Government.[38] This author believes the tendency to attribute the concept of "policymaking" to all three branches of government cause many to fuse the respective functions of the three branches. Therefore, it is understandable why 80 percent of the respondents to Questionnaire Two identified "judicial activism"—a term which, according to their responses to Questionnaire One, they believed to be inclusive of "judicial legislating"—as a term *imputed* to the Supreme Court.

It would follow then that the apparent contradiction of the respondents in pointing to the Court as engaging in judicial legislating through judicial activism (Questionnaire One), while responding thereafter that the term "judicial activism" is only imputed to the Court (Questionnaire Two), may not be so much a contradiction as a misunderstanding. The focus for the misunderstanding could be writings on the Supreme Court as a member of the tri-partite Federal system of government.

In summary, internal analysis of the empirical survey could suggest that external influences upon the Court are not held to be significant. This leads to the observation by this author that the function of judicial activism was regarded as an *internal* factor within the institution of the Supreme Court. As such, it was believed to be the result of influence within the Court, by or upon the Justices themselves.

Several of these "influences" are cited in Chapter II under the respective sections which explore the "Rule of Four," Certiorari, and judicial restraint. These examinations enabled us to see the

"Rule of Four" as an internal influence since, rather than there being a "Rule of Four" per se, there could also be a "rule of three", wherein a fourth Justice of the Court merely added his vote as a "courtesy".

Cue theory explains the role of Certiorari as an internal influence because it holds that, when certain "cues" exist, a Justice will grant Certiorari to a petition presented to the Court for review.

Judicial restraint acts an internal influence because of its balancing effect — i.e., the awareness on the part of the Court that, within its structure, there are limitations of institutional competency, as has been pointed out by Judge J. Skelly Wright. One manifest indication of such institutional limitation, for example, is found in Wright's observation: "Judgment in a particular case binds only the two parties."[39]

External influences upon the Supreme Court, as seen in the analysis of survey results, were not regarded as significant. However, as this author has shown, the function of judicial activism is directly linked to the internal *procedures* of the Court. It is from the relationship of the influences within, rather than from without, that the Supreme Court has had imputed to it the "appearance" of engaging in Judicial Legislating, and, with that, the "appearance" of engaging in Judicial Activism.

CONCLUSION

According to the working definition set forth earlier, judicial activism is any constitutional interpretation by the Supreme Court of the United States, within its power of original jurisdiction, in any case in which it decides, makes a policy formulation, or a ruling, by a majority or a minority of the Court. Judicial restraint, on the other hand, is defined as a limitation on any constitutional interpretation by the Supreme Court of the United States, within its power of original jurisdiction, in any case in which it decides, makes a policy formulation, or a ruling, by a majority or a minority of the Court.

From these definitions, and from the examination of the nature of judicial activism herein, it has been shown that the United States Supreme Court has not and does not venture outside its powers of original jurisdiction.

The findings of the empirical survey cited in Chapter III indicated that professors and students of political science tend to believe that the Supreme Court, in fact, does legislate. We also have seen how the respondents who expressed this belief may have been induced to accept such a view by the writings of legal and non-legal scholars.

Moreover, the other responses to Questionnaire One revealed a close second choice among the remaining respondents, who variously stated that "judicial activism" included judicial legislating, judicial legal policy, judicial restraint, and judicial administration. One is similarly able to conclude from reasons already cited that these responses were probably induced by the writings of legal and non-legal scholars.

The primary objective of this study, however, was to determine the influences upon and within the Court which led observers and critics to maintain that it does, in fact, legislate—i.e., that it does engage in judicial activism.

Earlier, the author conceded that the Court does engage in establishing ground-breaking precedent. This was found to be true because the Court, through such activity, merely exercises its power of original jurisdiction, an inherent power granted to the Court by Congress. However, the establishment of precedent by the Court through its exercise of original jurisdiction should not be confused with "judicial legislating". The sources and findings cited herein show this criticism of the Court to be fallacious — and without substance. On this very point, however, the professors and students responding to the second questionnaire did, in the main, agree: judicial activism is a term imputed to the Supreme Court.

At the same time, if these aggregate respondents, scholars, and critics of the Court believe the Court is engaging in judicial activism — and, therefore, "legislating" — why do they believe this? What is it about the Supreme Court as an institution that projects such an image? As we have seen in **Figure 3**, the image of the Court is the perceived outward manifestation of its inward functioning. Therefore, if there is some substance to the charge that the Court is practicing judicial activism, it derives from the appearance given by certain aspects of the Court's internal function.

Chapter II of this study dealt with the Court's function within the realm of its original jurisdiction granted by Congress. From this, we were able to see that the Court may give the appearance of practicing judicial activism because of four factors: (1) the "Rule of Four"; (2) 5-to-4 decisions and their effect on the Court's image; (3) the concept of "Certiorari"; and (4) judicial restraint. Each of these aspects were examined at some length as a possible example of a function of judicial activism within the Supreme Court.

The major source of confusion on this issue, which neither the aggregate respondents nor writers and critics of the Court appear to address, is the concept of the Court's *discretion*. As we have seen, this inherent power, so adeptly used by the Court, was granted to it by Congress on the Court's own motion in 1925, through the Judges' Bill. It is through the exercise of this grant of discretion that the Supreme Court is able to achieve today much of what makes it a strong and viable part of the *tri-partite* federal system of government. Additionally, it is through this discretion that the Supreme Court is able to give *balance* to its legal policy formulations. In keeping with its own views of balance in legal policy promulgations, we have seen how the Court relies on judicial restraints to prevent its encroachment on the other branches of federal government.

Finally, it is also through its exercise of discretion and its own internal function that the Supreme Court appears to be engaging in judicial activism.

From the foregoing, this author concludes: there is no *philosophy of judicial activism* as practiced by Justices of the United States Supreme Court. Instead, there is merely a philosophy of judicial activism as imputed to the Supreme Court by persons who are apparently unfamiliar with the significance of certain functions of the Court and the judicial process of the United States.

DOCUMENTATION

[1] William F. Swindler, *Court and Constitution in the 20th Century: The New Legality, 1932-1968* (New York and Indianapolis: The Bobbs-Merrill Company, Inc., 1970), p. 195.

[2] Wallace Mendelson, ed., *The Supreme Court: Law and Discretion* (New York and Indianapolis: The Bobbs-Merrill Company, Inc., 1967), p. 3.

[3] Lon Fuller, *The Law in Quest of Itself* (Boston: Beacon Press, 1942), p. 56.

[4] Sir Ernest Barker, *Social Contract* (London: Oxford University Press, 1970), pp. 147-166. See section on "David Hume".

[5] Bernard Schwartz, *The Bill of Rights: A Documentary History* (New York: McGraw Hill Book Company, 1971), p. 22. In speaking of the English in their short experience with a Republican Policy (1649-1660), Schwartz provides essential background for the early beginnings of constitutional law: "Even before the execution of the king, in contemplation of such an event, the Council of the Army had presented in January, 1649, a sketch of a Republican Constitution known as the *Agreement of the People*. This document has been well characterized as a landmark in the history of constitutional theory. As the first written organic instrument in Anglo-American history, it suggestively anticipated many of the fundamentals of the later American Constitution. In particular, it was

based upon the essential notion of a constitution as laying down significant checks upon the power of government itself."

[6] William F. Swindler, *Magna Carta: Legend and Legacy* (New York: The Bobbs-Merrill Company, Inc., 1965).

[7] Charles Reich, "Mr. Justice Black and the Living Constitution," *Harvard Law Review* 76 (February 1963): 673.

[8] This discussion occured during a personal interview by the author with the late Mr. Justice Hugo L. Black, in May, 1969.

[9] J. Skelly Wright, "The Role of the Supreme Court in a Democratic Society — Judicial Activism or Restraint?," *Cornell Law Review* 54 (November 1968): 27-28.

[10] Alpheus Thomas Mason, "Judicial Activism — Old and New," *Virginia Law Review* 55 (April 1969): 389.

[11] Charles Warren, "Legislative and Judicial Attacks on the Supreme Court of the United States — A History of the 25th Section of the Judiciary Act," *The American Law Review* 47 (January-February 1913).

[12] Tom Braden, "Two Ways to Argue Executive Privilege," *Washington Post*, 24 March 1973, p. A17.

[13] *United States vs. Carolene Products Company*, 304 U.S. 144, Number 4, 1938, pp. 152-153. In commenting upon the Carolene Case, Professor Alpheus Thomas Mason stated in his article, "The New Activism": "It seems ironical that Justice Stone, an eloquent exponent of judicial self-restraint in the late 1920's and early 1930's, should have formulated in a footnote the theoretical foundations of today's judicial activism," p. 394.

[14] Melvin L. Wulf, "An Optimistic Appraisal: The Supreme Court's 1971-72 Term", *Civil Liberties*, October 1972, p. 1, col. 1.

[15] Ibid., p. 7.

[16] John P. Mackenzie, "Court Activism Becomes Issue," *Washington Post*, 29 May 1972, p. A27.

[17] *United States vs. Carolene Products Company*, 304 U.S. 144, Number 4, 1938, pp. 152-153.

[18] For a partial discussion of the 25th Section of the Judiciary Act of 1789, see footnote 11. See also: Harold C. Syrett, *American Historical Documents*, (New York: Barnes & Noble, Inc., 1960), p. 130. The Judiciary Act as a whole was affirmed by the Supreme Court in the case of *Maubury vs. Madison*, 1 Cranch 137, 1803, in which the Court upheld the 13th Section of the Act, which had the effect of affirming the Act as a whole. The Act of 1789 also expanded the basis of the Original Jurisdiction of the Supreme Court. The Act, which was read in part in the case of *Maubury vs. Madison*, provided: "*And be it further enacted*, That the Supreme Court shall have exclusive jurisdiction of all controversies of a civil nature, where a state is a party, except between a state and citizens of other states, or aliens, in which latter case it shall have original but not exclusive jurisdiction. And shall have exclusively all such jurisdiction of suits or proceedings against ambassadors, or other public ministers, or their domestics, or domestic servants, as a court of law can have or exercise consistently with the law of nations; and original, but not exclusive, jurisdiction of all suits brought by ambassadors, or other public ministers, or in which a consul, or vice consul, shall be a party. And the trial of issues in fact in the Supreme Court, in all actions at law against citizens of the United States, shall be a jury. The Supreme Court shall also have appellate jurisdiction from the circuit courts and courts of the several states, in the cases herein after specially provided for; and shall have power to issue writs of prohibition to the district courts, when proceedings as courts of admiralty and maritime, jurisdiction, and writs of mandamus, in such cases warranted, or persons holding office, under the authority of the United States."

[19] See Article Three, United States Constitution.

[20] Norman J. Small, Editor, and Lester S. Jayson, Supervising Editor, *The Constitution of the United States of America: Analysis and Interpretation* (Washington, D.C.: U.S. Government Printing

Office, 1964), 88th Congress, 1st Session, Senate, Document Number 39, Prepared by the Legislative Reference Service, Library of Congress, p. 564.

[21] Ibid., pp. 564-565.

[22] An Act passed the 68th Congress, Session II, Chapter 229, 1925.

[23] Wallace Mendelson, ed., *The Supreme Court: Law and Discretion* (New York and Indianapolis: The Bobbs-Merrill Company, Inc., 1967), pp. 101-132.

[24] Scholars and journalists have pointed out that, even when the Court does deny a Certiorari petition, it has the effect of affirming the decision of the lower court.

[25] *Rules of the Supreme Court of the United States* (Washington, D.C.: Government Printing Office, 1970), pp. 20-23.

[26] Joan Maisel Leiman, "The Rule of Four," *Columbia Law Review* 57 (November 1950), p. 975.

[27] Ibid.

[28] Ibid.

[29] Ibid., p. 976.

[30] Theodore Plucknett, *A Concise History of the Common Law* (Boston: Little, Brown & Company, 1956), p. 173.

[31] Sixty-Eighth Congress, Op. Cit., Section 238 of the Act provides: "... a direct review by the Supreme Court of an interlocutory of final judgment or decree of a district court may be had where it is so provided in the following Act or parts of Acts, and not otherwise...," p. 938.

[32] Sydney Ulmer, "The Decision to Grant or Deny Certiorari: Further Considerations of Cue Theory," *The Law and Society Review* 6 (May 1972), pp. 637-643.

[33] Ibid.

[34] Ibid.

[35] *Sweeny vs. New Hampshire*, 354 U.S. 254, 1957.

[36] J. Skelly Wright, "The Role of the Supreme Court in a Democratic Society — Judicial Activism or Restraint?," *Cornell Law Review* 54 (1968) :27-28.

[37] The approach to the "behavioral research" which was conducted for the purposes of this study was an outgrowth of several sources, among them Gordon Tullock's *The Organization of Inquiry* (Durham, N.C.: Duke University Press, 1966), Morris Rosenberg's *The Logic of Survey Analysis* (New York: Basic Books, Inc., 1968), the conceptual and practical framework of the Judicial Process Questionnaire, as modified by Professor Nikolaos Stavrou of the Department of Political Science, Howard University, and the author's own modifications of the research data in conformity with the foregoing guidance.

[38] Richard S. Wells and Joel B. Grossman, "The Concept of Judicial Policy-Making: A Critic," *Journal of Public Law* 15 (1966):308.

[39] J. Skelly Wright, "The Role of the Supreme Court in a Democratic Society — Judicial Activism or Restraint?," *Cornell Law Review* 54 (November 1968) 3-11.

SELECTED BIBLIOGRAPHY

Abraham, Henry J. *The Judicial Process*. New York: University Press, 1968.

____. The Judiciary. Boston: Allyn & Bacon, 1969.

Ardrey, Robert. *The Social Contract*. New York: A Delta Book, 1970.

Arnold, Thurman W. *The Symbols of Government*. New York: A Harbinger Book, 1962.

Austin, John. *The Austinian Theory of Law*. London: J. Murray, 1912.

____. *The Province of Jurisprudence Determined and the Uses of the Study of Jurisprudence*. New York: Moonday Press, 1954.

Becker, Theodore L. *Comparative Judicial Politics*. Chicago: Rand McNally & Company, 1970.

Benton, Thomas Hart. *Examination of the Dred Scott Case*. Kraus Reprint Company, 1857.

Berger, Raoul. *Congress vs. the Supreme Court*. Massachusetts: Harvard University Press, 1969.

Bickel, Alexander M. *The Supreme Court and the Idea of Progress*. New York: Harper & Row Publishers, 1970.

———. *The Least Dangerous Branch*. Indianapolis: The Bobbs-Merrill Company, Inc., 1962.

Black, Hugo L. *A Constitutional Faith*. New York: Alfred A. Knopf, 1968.

Cardozo, Benjamin N. *The Nature of the Judicial Process*. New Haven: Yale University Press, 1967.

Carpenter, William Seal. *Foundations of Modern Jurisprudence*. Appleton, Century-Crofts, Inc., 1958.

Corwin, Edward S. *The "Higher Law" Background of American Constitutional Law*. Ithaca & London: Cornell University Press, 1971.

Davis, Kenneth Culp. *Discretionary Justice*. Urbana: University of Illinois Press, 1971.

Dillard, Irving. *One Man's Stand for Freedom: Mr. Justice Black and the Bill of Rights: A Collection of His Supreme Court Opinions*. New York: Alfred A. Knopf, 1963.

Douglas, William O. *We the Judges*. New York: Doubleday & Company, Inc., 1956.

Ehrlich, H. W. *Ehrlich's Blackstone/1*. New York: Capricorn Books, 1959.

———. *Ehrlich's Blackstone/2*. New York: Capricorn Books, 1959.

Ernest, Morris L. *The Ultimate Power*. New York: Doubleday & Company, 1937.

Etzioni, Amitai. *The Active Society*. New York: The Free Press, 1968.

SELECTED BIBLIOGRAPHY

Forte, David. *The Supreme Court in American Politics: Judicial Activism vs. Judicial Restraint*. Boston: D.C. Heath Publishers, 1972.

Frank, John P. *Mr. Justice Black: The Man and His Opinions*. New York: Alfred A. Knopf, 1949.

Frankfurter, Felix. *Of Law and Life and Other Things that Matter*. Boston: Harvard University Press, 1965.

Frankfurter, Felix, and Landis, James M. *The Business of the Supreme Court*. New York: MacMillian, 1927.

Fuller, Lon. *The Law in Quest of Itself*. Boston: Beacon Press, 1942.

____. *Legal Fictions*. Stanford: Stanford University Press, 1967.

Griswold, Erwin N. *Law and Lawyers in the United States*. Cambridge: Harvard University Press, 1965.

Hadas, Moses. *The Basic Works of Cicero*. New York: The Modern Library, 1951.

____. *Livy: A History of Rome*. New York: The Modern Library, 1951.

Hamilton, Alexander. *The Federalist Papers*. New York: A Mentor Book, 1961.

Hand, Learned. *The Bill of Rights*. New York: Atheneum, 1968.

Hart, H. L. A. *The Concept of Law*. London: Oxford University Press, 1961.

Holmes, Oliver Wendell. *The Common Law*. Boston: Little, Brown & America Company, 1963.

Hughes, Charles Evans. *The Supreme Court of the United States*. New York: Columbia University Press, 1928.

Jackson, Robert H. *The Struggle for Judicial Supremacy*. New York: Vintage Press, 1941.

Jacob, Herbert. *Justice in Ameica*. Boston: Little, Brown & Company, 1965.

Kauper, Paul G. *Religion and the Constitution*. Louisiana: Louisiana State University Press, 1964.

Kelsen, Hans. *General Theory of Law and State*. New York: Russell & Russell, 1961.

Konefsky, Samuel J. *The Constitutional World of* Mr. Justice Frankfurter. New York: MacMillan, 1949.

Krislov, Samuel. *The Supreme Court and Political Freedom*. New York: Free Press, 1968.

Kurland, Phillip B. *Felix Frankfurter on the Supreme Court*. Cambridge: Harvard University Press, 1970.

Levy, Beryl H. *Our Constitution: Tool or Testament*? New York: Kennikat Press, 1965.

Little, David. *Religion, Order and Law*. New York: Torchbooks, 1969.

Lloyd, Dennis. *The Idea of Law*. Maryland: Penguin Books, 1964.

Locke, John et al. *Social Contract*. Oxford: Oxford University Press, 1970.

Lowie, Robert H. *The Origin of the State*. New York: Russell & Russell, Inc., 1962.

McCoskey, Robert G. *Essays in Constitutional Law*. New York: Vintage Press, 1957.

Maine, Henry. *Ancient Law*. New York: Everyman's Library, 1965.

SELECTED BIBLIOGRAPHY

Mendelson, Wallace. *The Supreme Court: Law and Discretion*. Indianapolis: The Bobbs-Merrill Company, Inc., 1967.

____. *Justice Black and Frankfurter: Conflict in the Court*. Chicago: University of Chicago Press, 1961.

Miller, Charles A. *The Supreme Court and the Use of History*.

Morris, Clarence. *The Great Legal Philosophers*. Philadelphia: University of Pennsylvania Press, 1959.

Murphy, Paul L. *The Constitution in Crisis Times*. New York: Harper & Row, 1972.

Murphy, Walter. *Elements of Judicial Strategy*. Chicago: University of Chicago Press, 1954.

Myrdal, Gunner. *The American Dilemma*. New York: Harper & Row, 1962.

Padover, Saul K. *To Secure these Blessings*. New York: Kraus Reprint Company, 1962.

Plucknett, Theodore, F. T. *A Concise History of the Common Law*. Boston: Little, Company, 1956.

Post, Gordon C. *An Introduction to the Law*. Englewood Cliffs: Prentice-Hall, Inc., 1963.

Pound, Roscoe. *Jurisprudence*. St. Paul: West Publishing Company, 1959.

Pritchett, C. Herman. *The American Constitutional System*. New York: McGraw-Hill, 1967.

Reich, Charles A. *The Greening of America*. New York: Random House, 1970.

Roche, John P. *Courts and Rights: The Supreme Court in Action*. New York: Random House, 1966.

Rodell, Fred. *Nine Men*. New York: Vintage Press, 1955.

Schubert, Glendon. *The Judicial Mind*. Evanston: Northwestern University Press, 1965.

———. *Dispassionate Justice*. Indianapolis: The Bobbs-Merrill Company, Inc., 1969.

Schwartz, Bernard. *The Bill of Rights*. Lawyers Literary Club, 1971.

Shapiro, Martin M. *The Supreme Court and Public Policy*. Illinois: Scott, Foresman, 1969.

Strakosch, Henry E. *State Absolutism and the Rule of Law*. Australia: Sydney University Press, 1967.

Strickland, Stephan. *Hugo Black and the Supreme Court*. Indianapolis: The Bobbs-Merrill Company, Inc., 1967.

Swindler, William F. *Court and Constitution in the 20th Century*. Indianapolis: The Bobbs-Merrill Company, Inc., 1969.

———. *Magna Carta*. Indianapolis: The Bobbs-Merrill Company, Inc., 1965.

Syrett, Harold C. *American Historical Documents*. New York: Barnes & Noble, 1960.

Ten Broek, Jacobus. *Equal Under Law*. New York: Colliers, 1965.

Willoughby, Westel W. *The Fundamental Concepts of Public Law*. New York: MacMillan, 1931.

Wilson, Woodrow. *The State*. Boston: D.C. Heath & Company, 1918.

Wormser, Rene A. *The Story of the Law*. New York: Simon & Schuster, 1962.

LAWS REVIEWS

Leiman, Joan Maisel. "The Rule of Four." *Columbia Law Review* 57 (1950).

Mason, Alpheus Thomas. "Judicial Activism — Old and New." *Virginia Law Review* 55 (1969).

Reich, Charles. "Mr. Justice Black and the Living Constitution." *Harvard Law Review* 76 (1963).

Wells, Richard S., and Grossman, Joel B. "The Concept of Judicial Policy-Making: A Critic." *Journal of Public Law* 15 (1966).

Wright, J. Skelly. "The Role of the Supreme Court in a Democratic Society: Judicial Activism or Restraint?". *Cornell Law Review* 54 (1968).

CASES

Adams vs. California, 332 U.W. 46 (1947).

Brown vs. School Board of Topeka, Kansas, 347 U.S. 483 (1954).

Maubury vs. Madison, 1 Cranch 137 (1803).

Plessy vs. Ferguson, 163 U.S. 537 (1896).

Sweeny vs. New Hampshire, 354 U.S. 254 (1957).

U.S. vs. Carolene Products Company, 304 U.S. 144 (1938).

CONGRESSIONAL STATUTES

Fifty-First Congress, 11th sess., ch. 517, p. 829 (1891).

First Congress, Judiciary Act (1789).

Sixty-Eighth Congress, 11th sess., ch. 229 (1925).

Twenty-Eighth United States Code Annotated, sec. 41.

JOURNALS

Gibbs, Jack P. "Definitions of Law and Empirical Questions." *Law and Society Review* 2:429-446.

Ulmer, Sydney. "The Decision to Grant or Deny Certiorari: Further Considerations of Cue Theory." *Law and Society Review* 6 (May 1972) :637-643.

MAGAZINES

Methvin, Eugene H.. "The Supreme Court Changes Course." *Readers Digest*, October 1972.

"No-Nonsense Innovation." *Time Magazine*, Law Section, 19 April 1971.

NEWSPAPERS

Cummerford, Edward F. "Judicial Jumble 'Activism as Threat to Government of Laws and Not of Men.'" *Wall Street Journal*, 22 April 1968.

Mackenzie, John P. "Court Activism Becomes Issue." *Washington Post*, 29 May 1972.

Wulf, Melvin L. "An Optimistic Appraisal of the Supreme Court's 1971-72 Term." *Civil Liberties*, October 1972, pp. 1, 4.

REPORTS

American Political Science Association, 68th Annual Meeting Program. Washington Hilton Hotel, Washington, D.C. 5-9 September 1972.

Annual Report of the Director of the Administrative Office of the U.S. Courts, 1948-71.

Rules of the Supreme Court of the United States. Washington, D.C., U.S. Government Printing Office, 1970.

Task Force Reports: *The Courts*: The Task Force on the Administration of Justice. The President's Commission on Law Enforcement and Administration of Justice. Washington, D.C., U.S. Government Printing Office, 1967.

LETTERS

Letter from The Research Department, G & C Merriam Company, publishers of Merriam-Webster Dictionaries, pertaining to a definition of the term "judicial activism" in a forthcoming edition of Webster's 3rd International Dictionary. The Letter, written from its Research Department, also included statements as to the reason the concept had not been defined previously. November 18, 1971.

Letter from West Publishing Company, publisher of Black's Law Dictionary, pertaining to its "legal" definition of the concept of judicial activism. 24 November 1971.

Letter from Nikolaos Stavrou, Professor of Political Science, Howard University, Department of Political Science. Letter concerning the conceptual and practical framework of the judicial process questionnaire proposed by the author. 24 November 1971.

Letter from Judge William B. Jones, U.S. District Court of District of Columbia, pertaining to the source of several speeches made by members of the ABA Panel, "Law and Layman Program:

Courts — Traditional or Activist?", a program conducted on August 14, 1972 by the ABA Section of Judicial Administration.

PAPERS

"From Warren to Burger: The Rise and Decline of Substantive Equal Protection," Wallace Mendelson, Department of Government, University of Texas, Austin. Paper presented to a Section of the September 8, 1972 Annual Meeting of the American Political Science Association. The paper was later published in the December 1972 issue of *The American Political Science Review*, Volume LXVI, Number 4, p. 1226-1233.

"The Conservatism of American Legal Historiography," Morton J. Horwitz, Professor Law, Harvard Univeristy Law School. Paper presented to a Section on DIRECTIONS IN AMERICAN LEGAL HISTORY, November 4, 1972, at Williamsburg Lodge and Conference Center.

"Justices Black and Douglas: The Judicial Function and the Scope of Constitutional Liberties," Tinsley Yarbrough. Paper presented in November, 1972 at the 44th Annual Meeting, Southern Political Science Association.

DISSERTATIONS

Synder, Eloise C. "A Quantitative Analysis of Supreme Court Opinions from 1921 to 1953: A Study of the Responses of an Institution Engaged in Resolving Social Conflict." Michigan: University Microfilms, Inc., 1956.

Sprague, John. "Voting Patterns on the United States Supreme Court: Cases in Federalism, 1889-1959." Michigan: University Microfilms, Inc., 1964.

PROGRAMS AND CONFERENCES

American Bar Association, Section on Judicial Administration, San Francisco, California, 14-17 August 1972. Panel Discussion: "Come Judge the Judges," a part of the "Law and Layman" Program, "Courts — Traditional or Activist?". The panelists were John Mackenzie, Reporter, *Washington Post*; Moses Lasky, *Esquire*, Attorney, San Francisco, California; Dean Robert E. Sullivan, Law School, University of Montana, Missoula, Montana; and Charles Gould, Publisher, *San Francisco Examiner*, San Francisco, California.

American Bar Foundation, Editor, Chicago, Illinois, August 18, 1972. Conference pertaining to the status of the Concept of Judicial Activism within the American Bar Foundation, in terms of ongoing research.

CBS NEWS SPECIAL: "Justice Black and the Bill of Rights." Columbia Broadcasting System. The actual interview, by Eric Sevaried and Martin Agronsky, was televised December 3, 1968, 10:00-11:00 P.M., EST.

Horwitz, Professor Morton J. American Society for Legal History, November 4, 1972.

Jones, Judge William B. Leader, Panel Discussion, Section on Judicial Administration, American Bar Association. Judge Jones is a member of the U.S. District Court, District of Columbia.

Swartz, Richard. Dean, State University of New York Law School. Annual Meeting, Law and Society Association, August 29, 1972, New Orleans, Louisiana.

PERSONAL INTERVIEW

Black, Justice Hugo L., United States Supreme Court. Conducted by the author on May 16, 1969 in the Supreme Court Chambers of the late Mr. Justice Black. The interview elicited Mr. Justice Black's personal opinions on the concept of "Judicial Activism". The author elected to interview Mr. Justice Black because many scholars had identified him as the "center-most actor" within the realm of an "Active Judiciary", particularly in his role as a member of the United States Supreme Court.